THE WESTIN MAUI

No. 1 Capitol District, Honolulu, Hawaii 96813

Library of Congress Catalog Card Number 88-84145

ISBN 1-877690-00-7

First Printing, May 1989

Series Editor: George Fuller

Design by Steve Shrader Graphic Design, Honolulu, Hawaii

Typesetting by Typehouse Hawaii, Honolulu, Hawaii

Printed through Times Editions Pte., Singapore

Printed in Singapore

THE WESTIN MAUI

Text by
JERRY HOPKINS

Photography by
WILLIAM WATERFALL

Hemmeter Publishing
1989

CONTENTS

INTRODUCTION
PAGE 15

MAUI
The Valley Isle
PAGE 21

IN OLD HAWAII
Tales of Polynesian Supermen
PAGE 33

MEN OF GOD
& SUGAR KINGS
Calling It Sinful, Turning It Green
PAGE 39

THE PLANNER
& THE HOTEL KEEPER
Real Estate, Statehood & Golf
PAGE 45

THE VISIONARY
Fantasy, Romance & Luxury
PAGE 51

THE VISION
You Must Be Overwhelmed
PAGE 59

Christopher B. Hemmeter
Developer of the Westin Maui

INTRODUCTION

loha!

It is with great pleasure that I welcome you to the Westin Maui Hotel, one of the world's truly "Grand Resorts." I take special care, and pride, in the design and construction of a Hemmeter hotel. For me, a resort destination is successful only if it satisfies the most exacting criteria.

First and foremost, it must create a sense of experience. People want more than a room and a bed. Today's traveler is looking for revival, for newness, for the unexpected. The impact must be greater than the sum of the many parts.

It is my hope that we have created that forever memorable experience through this hotel. Five swimming pools on three levels, connected by water slides . . . waterfalls and romantic grottoes . . . the beachside ambience of Polynesia blending with the classic lines of Colonial Hawaiian architecture . . . a priceless art collection from Europe and Asia.

We have created a jewel, set in a mounting of breathtaking beauty—with its brilliant white sand beach, cool trade winds, offshore islands, and the best sunsets in the Pacific.

However, a successful resort must also "recreate," for recreation is the truest of all experiences. It must allow its guests to revive emotions and feelings that have been dormant, to refresh the mind and soul, to give fresh life, to reanimate, to divert and amuse.

When a hotel allows its guests to create a new experience and at the same time recreate old feelings of excitement, it is a winner.

This book includes an anecdotal history of the property on which the hotel sits—from legendary times forward, through the history of pre-contact Hawaii (when a small village of grass houses was not far from where the hotel is today), the arrival of the missionaries, the development of this region as a sugar plantation, and then as Hawaii's first planned destination resort.

This book also presents the hotel itself: the hotel as art and the hotel as art gallery. At the same time, we are attempting to illustrate and explain one of the world's largest private collections of Asian and European art—more than 5,000 pieces in all, stretching back 6,000 years into antiquity.

Once again, let me welcome you to the Westin Maui, truly a "Grand Resort."

Enjoy!

A stairway of electric stars and gleaming brass leads guests to the Sound of the Falls, a restaurant for elegant dining nestled by Kaanapali Beach. Waiters and flamingos are standing by.

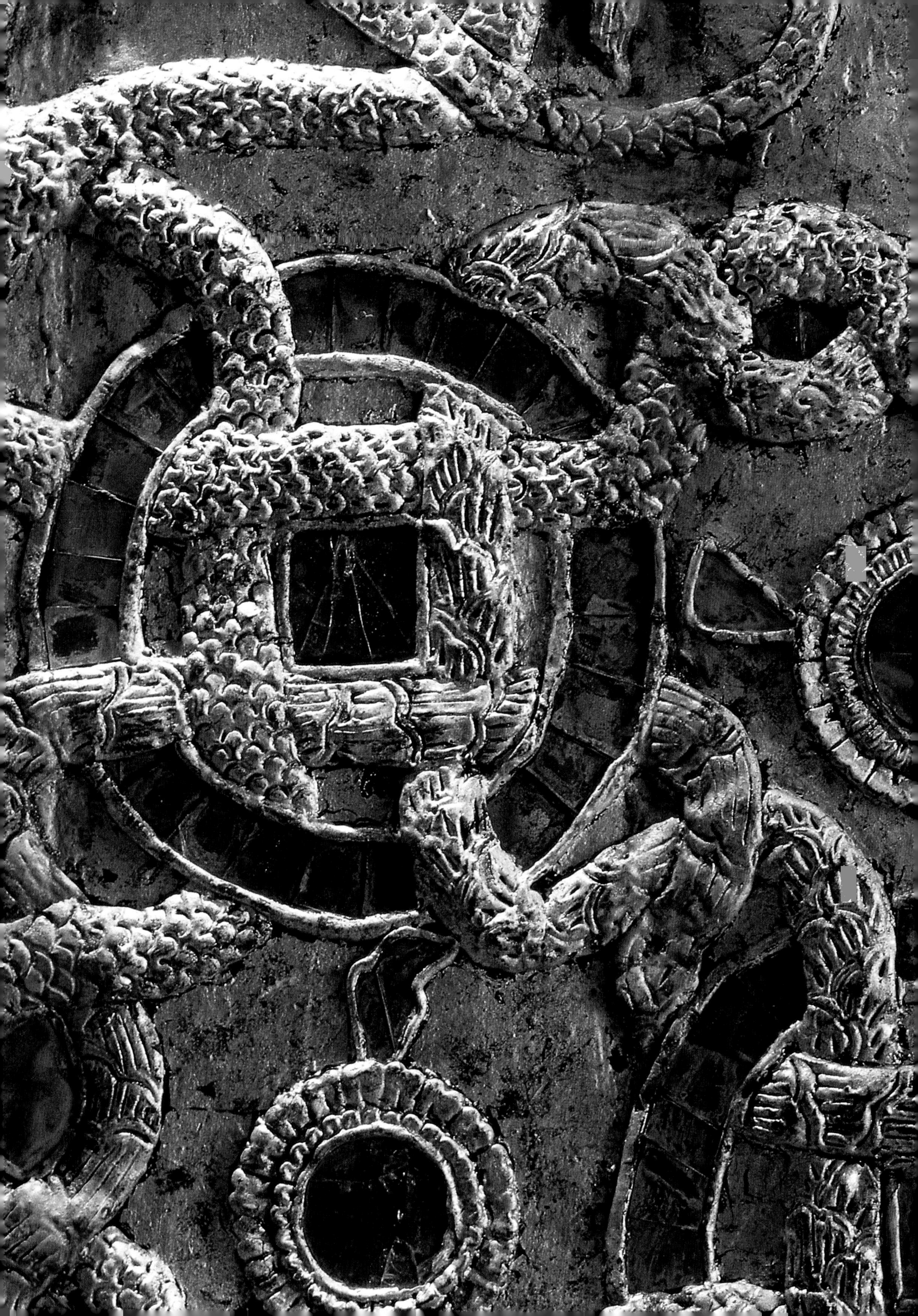

From a faraway temple in Thailand, destroyed by the relentless test of time, an elaborately carved ceiling panel is transported to Hawaii for display in a grand hotel.

The rising sun casts wake-up rays into the moonscape of Haleakala Crater, Maui's highest peak. It is here that one of the island's legendary demi-gods captured the sun with a lasso to make the day longer.

The warm Pacific surf comes washing in like champagne, pushing its bubbles over the rattling rocks in a small cove near Makena, on Maui's Gold Coast.

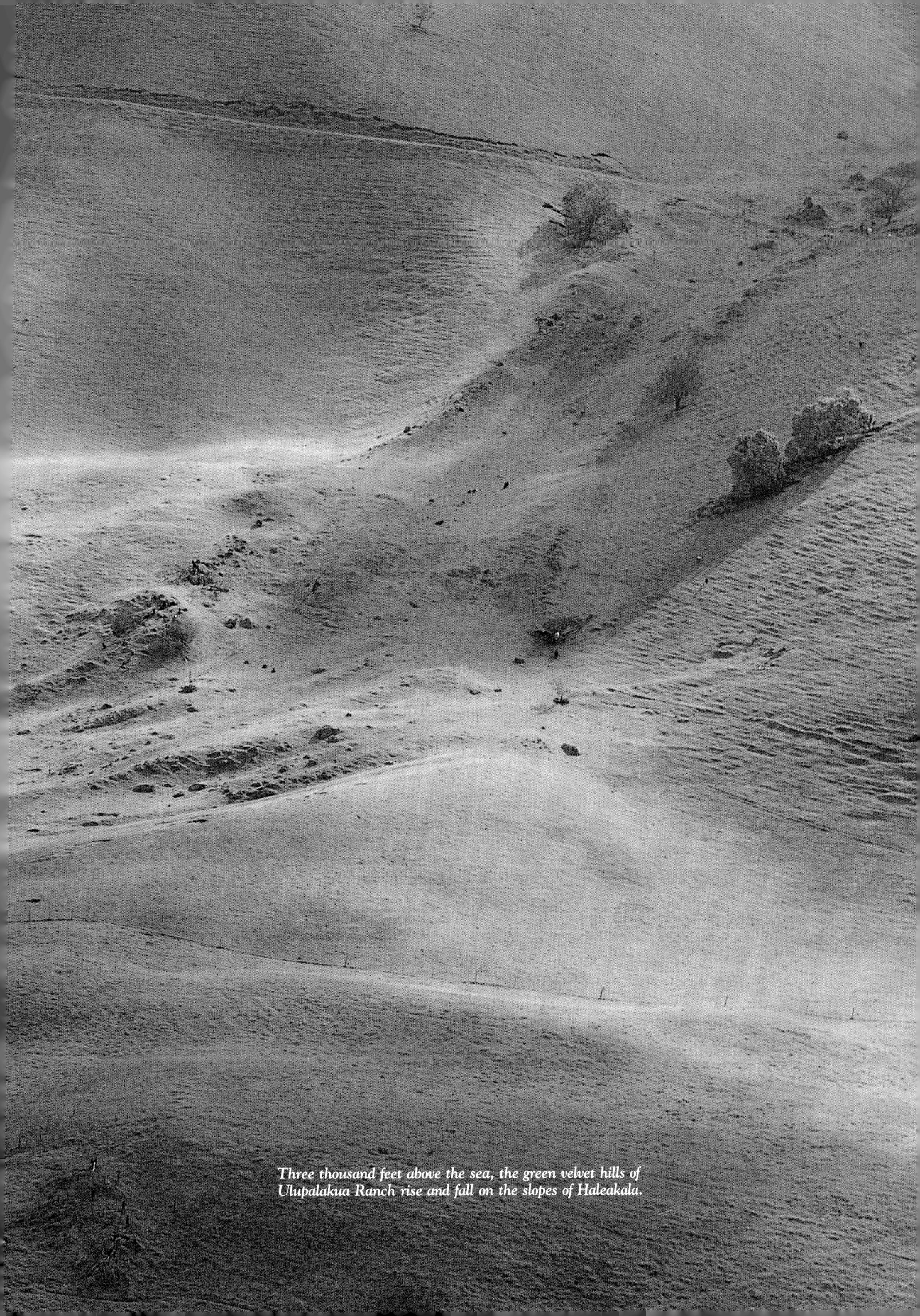

Three thousand feet above the sea, the green velvet hills of Ulupalakua Ranch rise and fall on the slopes of Haleakala.

IN OLD HAWAII

Tales of Polynesian Supermen

The Hawaiians lived in Kaanapali in small villages scattered along the coast. They grew taro where the streams came down from the mountains and caught fish in the ocean beside a long, wide beach.

Here, they gathered under the kiawe trees in small groups by the light of burning candlenut to listen to the *kupuna,* or oldtimers, tell stories.

A favorite subject was Maui, the playful but powerful demi-god for whom the island was named. His many mythical adventures included pushing up the sky, getting fire from a mudhen, and pulling up islands from the sea, but the story most often told concerned his snaring of the sun.

According to this popular legend, the sun moved too quickly across the sky, giving Hawaiians too little time to complete their daily chores. So Maui made a giant lasso from coconut fiber and climbed to the island's highest spot to await the sun's appearance over the morning horizon. He planned to catch the sun with his rope and hold it in place to lengthen the day.

One of Maui's friends laughed, and stood nearby to watch him fail. After Maui accomplished his mighty task, he chased the man, catching him on the Kaanapali coast. Following a brief struggle, the man was changed into a great black rock called Puu Kekaa, site of today's Sheraton Maui Hotel.

In time, this rock was also called a *leinaa ka uhane,* or "soul's leap." When someone in ancient Hawaii lay dying, his or her soul left the body to search for a passage to death. If the individual had led a peaceful life, the soul found its way to Puu Kekaa, where it was met by the gods. All the islands reportedly had at least one such place from which the soul could make its final leap.

Kaulu was another demi-god credited with magical feats. According to legend, he was born in the form of a rope, but as a human with strong hands, he created the surf by breaking the waves, made one long dog into many small dogs, and made the sea salty by swallowing it and spitting it out.

To many he was known as the Breadfruit Boy, because he uprooted his father's breadfruit saplings. Breadfruit was a staple necessary for the ancient village's survival, so Kaulu was punished severely. He was set adrift from Makaiwa

(Opposite page) A lone dancer's chant reverberates from the awesome cliffs of Lanai. The ancient message is thrown to Kaanapali Beach in the distance.

Beach south of where the Hyatt Regency Maui is today. Before shoving Kaulu's canoe into the sea, the village chief armed the boy with a sacred spear.

Some time later, landing on nearby Lanai, he found a community under the control of evil spirits, which he chased away. Kaulu then took the spear and drew a circle around the village, protecting it from future harm. Returning to Kaanapali, he was greeted with aloha and to this day, whenever new buildings or businesses are dedicated in Hawaii, a lei of the fragrant maile vine is draped across the entrance, symbolizing the protective circle of Kaulu.

The "true" history of Kaanapali is blended with such tales, because the stories of great chiefs and their accomplishments were told by the same storytellers, who learned them from the storytellers who came before.

Even well into the 20th Century there were those who could recite genealogies and chants going back hundreds and hundreds of years. And there were those who were skilled in the art of *apo,* or, literally, "catching" the spoken word. Men would chant without break for two or three hours, only to be followed by the *apo,* who repeated the entire recitation without missing a word.

The ancient Hawaiian was remarkable in many ways. Wave after wave of these people came, traveling thousands of miles in primitive canoes, without navigational instruments, led in their search for a new home by birds and dolphins, prevailing winds and ocean currents, shifting clouds and, most reliably, stars.

The first arrived from the Marquesas Islands, more than 2,000 miles to the southeast, between 500 and 800 A.D. Successive migrations came from the Society Islands, primarily Tahiti and Bora Bora, between 1100 and 1300 A.D.

A strict caste system was established, with a select group of *alii,* or nobility, who earned power through bloodline, dominating the *makaanana,* or commoners. All were governed by a rigid set of laws known as *kapu* (a variation of the Tahitian word *taboo*). Penalty for violating one of these laws generally was death by being strangled, stoned, buried or burned.

The people lived in houses made of grass and sticks in what was, essentially, a stone age civilization. There was no wheel. There was no pottery. Wars were fought with spears and clubs.

But this was not a simple society. There was a pantheon of gods and goddesses as humanly complicated and outrageous as those found in ancient Rome or Greece. And because it was an oral culture, with no written language, an extensive "library" of chants existed, including one called the *Kumulipo.* This was a story of creation that was 2,000 lines long, and went back to the cosmos in time. Scholars say it is as sophisticated as any other story of creation from anywhere else in the world.

In the 18th Century, great battles were fought as the chiefs from other islands waged bloody, hand-to-hand combat for control of Maui. One of these chiefs was Kahekili, who was tattooed a solid black from head to foot on his right side, a sign of his ferocity. His whole company of warrior chiefs and household companions were tattooed in the same way.

Kahekili was known to be fearless. As a young man, his favorite pastime was

said to be diving from tall cliffs. One of his favorite cliffs was Puu Kekaa in Kaanapali, where crowds of natives collected from the small village nearby to watch their chief propel himself into the boiling surf.

Kahekili was best known as a fierce warrior. Once, after a mighty battle, he built a house of skulls and bones to remind his enemies that the same fate was quickly theirs if they dared step out of line.

Kahekili died, unchallenged, leaving a kingdom that included all of Maui, Molokai, Lanai and Oahu divided between a brother and son. Soon those two were fighting and the brother was killed. Then a chief from the Big Island, who came to be called Kamehameha the Great, defeated the surviving heir. By conquering all the other islands as well, Kamehameha unified Hawaii for the first time. Today, a state holiday honors his name.

For a while, Kamehameha remained in Lahaina, which became the first capital of the island chain. When he died in 1819, he was succeeded by his favorite wife, Kaahumanu, and his first-born son through another wife, Liholiho, who became known as Kamehameha II.

The first white men came 40 years before, in 1878, and after that explorers, traders and whalers arrived in large numbers, changing Hawaii forever. Traders stripped the mountains of their sandalwood forests to sell to China. The same sailors brought guns, alcohol and venereal disease.

At Kaahumanu's urging, the 21-year-old king broke the *kapu* which kept men from eating with women. He then ordered that all *heiau* (temples) and godlike images be destroyed throughout the kingdom. The traditional Hawaiian culture lay shattered, like broken shells upon the beach.

Tranquility reigned in Lahaina in the mid-1820s,
from a drawing by Robert Dampier.

(Following pages) Male dancers perform the hula with feathered gourd rattles and dog-tooth anklets, as pictured here by the Russian artist Louis Choris during his visit to the Sandwich Islands in 1816.

MEN OF GOD & SUGAR KINGS

Calling It Sinful, Turning It Green

The early Congregationalist missionaries were well-established on three other islands before they came to Maui, in 1824. At that time, the native village of Lahaina stretched along a mile and a half of the rocky coastline, where there were about 700 grass houses with an estimated 2,300 souls.

Then, as now, Lahaina was the "big city" for West Maui, and Kaanapali was "country," with only a few small villages. In 1834, it was decided to start a circuit of "missionary out stations" and the first was built near Kekaa, about where the Maui Eldorado is today.

Within a few years an adobe school house was added, with another small home for the teacher. There was an extra room for the overnight accommodation of the missionary who came each weekend to preach.

For the first nine years, until 1843, the pastor was the Reverend Ephraim Clark, a frail and scholarly man who also taught at the Lahainaluna Mission School (still in operation and the oldest school west of the American Rocky Mountains), where he prepared classroom texts in the Hawaiian language.

The reverend taught a Bible class and Sabbath School and delivered two sermons on Sunday at the Kaanapali station. In reports sent back to mission headquarters in Boston, he spoke of "lewdness" and indicated that it was difficult to teach his students and members of the congregation such things as modesty, hard work and punctuality.

Clark's successor was John Emerson, who was youthful and handsome but no less temperate or severe. In 1846, he wrote, "Nothing of a peculiarly marked or very interesting character has occurred among the little church and people of Kaanapali during the past two years." He then went dryly on to say that there had been an epidemic 12 months earlier, making all in the district ill, killing hundreds.

Disease was becoming commonplace, introduced by visiting sailors to a vulnerable native population whose immune system could not fight off the strange assault.

(Opposite page) Pioneer Mill, surrounded by waving fields of cane.

Clark and Emerson also noted that the Kaanapali region had little rainfall, so crops were unpredictable. Consequently, many natives drifted into Lahaina, which during the mid-1800s became Hawaii's most popular whaling port.

In 1859 the number of ships dropping anchor offshore reached 549, bringing an average of 200 sailors per ship, or 110,000 during the year. Hawaii was experiencing its first tourist boom. Grog shops were commonplace along what is now Front Street and the ministers fought public drunkenness.

In time, the whaling grounds between Alaska and Hawaii were depleted. Whalebone used in corsets was replaced by more plentiful and cheaper celluloid and steel. San Francisco developed as an alternate port to Lahaina. The death blow came in 1859, when petroleum was discovered in Pennsylvania. Its derivative, kerosene, was cleaner, brighter, and cheaper than whale oil for use in lamps.

Surprisingly, it was sleepy Kaanapali that took up much of the economic slack.

As early as 1840, David Malo, one of the first great Hawaiian scholars to graduate from Lahainaluna, experimented with growing sugar cane in the Lahaina and Kaanapali area. Others joined him and when island laws were changed to allow aliens to lease land for as long as 50 years, and then, in 1850, to buy property on the same terms as native Hawaiians, the first sugar companies were formed.

Success was elusive at first, but the American Civil War created a new market. Much of the sugar consumed in the North was cultivated in the South and this source was cut off. In 1859, the islands exported 1.8 million pounds of sugar. Midway through the hostilities, in 1864, the total was 10.4 million pounds.

A reciprocity treaty between the islands and the United States, signed in 1876, allowed Hawaiian sugar to enter the U.S. duty-free and within ten years, the total had increased to 171 million pounds.

Henry Hackfield was a German immigrant who started a small waterfront store in Honolulu. Acquiring land on Kauai and Maui, Hackfield served the sugar trade—at first providing labor and supplies, then capital, and, finally, serving as sales agent and lobbyist.

The Rev. Ephraim Clark, first missionary to preach in Kaanapali, sits sternly with his wife Mary for formal portraits, ca. 1850.

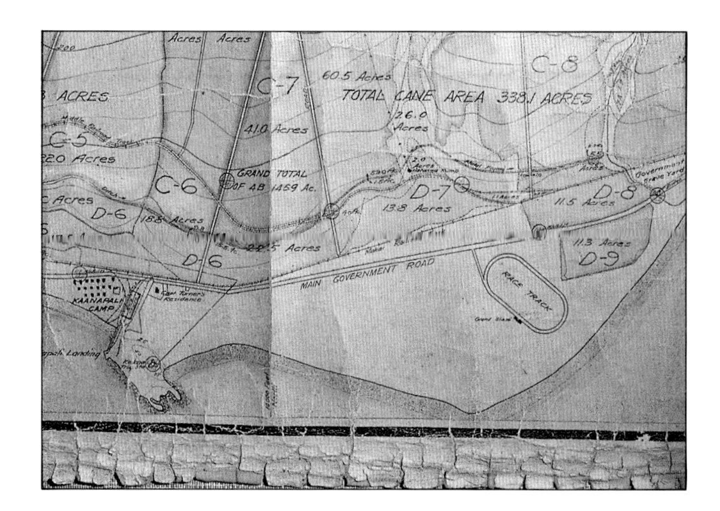

As the monarchy ended (in 1893) and Hawaii was given territorial status (in 1898), Hackfield grew rich and powerful, with varied interests on all the islands. He and a few others controlled the sugar industry by the turn of the century, providing or obtaining the capital the planters needed.

For Hackfield, history swung the other way during World War One, when German-owned businesses in the U.S. had their assets seized by the federal government. Hackfield was sold to a group of non-German businessmen and the name was changed to the patriotic sounding American Factors. And the firm's retail clothing store, B. F. Ehlers, became Liberty House.

Under the new management, a modern village grew up where the grass houses of Kekaa once stood. A warehouse the size of a football field was built adjacent to Black Rock, where the Sheraton cottages are today. Between that and the site of the Maui Eldorado were 20 cottages for the men who loaded sugar onto ships offshore.

Large tanks for fuel oil and molasses were on what is now the eighth green of the Royal Kaanapali Golf Course and the Sheraton's upper parking lot. Between the Sheraton and the Kaanapali Beach Hotel sites were feeding pens, where cattle were fattened with shredded pineapple skins and cores.

To the south, toward the mountains from today's Maui Marriott and Hyatt Regency, was a race track, a festive place on Kamehameha Day, when the island's fastest horses were raced. Nearby was a small air field used by crop dusters and the first commercial planes.

Kaanapali was now a great, wide sheet of waving, bladed green, divided by red clay cane haul roads and a railroad that ran all the way to Lahaina. Fertilizers had been introduced to the poor Kaanapali soil and artesian wells brought water.

Suddenly the fortunes of King Sugar reversed, when in 1934 the U.S. Congress enacted a law which ignored pre-territorial duty-free sugar agreements and reduced raw sugar imports to allow for increasing production of beet sugar from Colorado.

The Pioneer Sugar Mill would still be operating 50 years later, but the handwriting was on the sand. Sleepy little Kaanapali was headed for another upheaval.

A rare map of Kaanapali, ca. 1910, showing a race track and government graveyard (right) and miles of rail line connecting the cane fields with the sugar warehouse and loading dock (left).

(Following pages) In 1960, Kaanapali Beach lies waiting—its ancient history wiped away, and the excitement of a fantasy resort soon to become reality. Black Rock pokes into the ocean to the right. The site of the Westin Maui lies beyond.

sites were not preserved. There was no fishing or boating to speak of.

But the location was perfect in other ways. The steep West Maui mountains protected the area from clouds, heavy rain and strong trade winds. Rainfall averaged only 16 inches annually and temperatures stayed in the 70s.

The islands of Molokai and Lanai lay just offshore, offering dazzling postcard views with heart-warming sunsets to end the day. Only a few miles away was the 19th Century whaling village of Lahaina, the only town of its kind and size anywhere in the island chain. Lahaina clearly needed work, but the potential was there.

The report came in. Tourism in Kaanapali was not only feasible, but advisable. In 1956, at a luau celebration on the beach, it was decided to start the first, $10 million phase of the development.

Eleven hotel sites were blocked off, offering beachfronts averaging a generous 650 feet (compared to 400 feet fronting the Royal Hawaiian Hotel in Waikiki). A thousand rooms were projected by 1960. A marina was to be built where the Hyatt Regency Maui and part of the golf course are today.

If some of the plans were changed—and the marina was never built—the impact was everything that was hoped for. *The Maui News* was correct when it said that, "Lahaina and the entire island of Maui are poised on the brink of the most gigantic economic development of any community in Hawaii; that the West Side resort project will touch off a prosperity era that will affect all areas of the Valley Island and everyone residing thereon."

Dudley Child wanted his company, InterIsland Resorts, to develop the first hotel in Kaanapali.

Child was a native of Honolulu and a graduate of Punahou School, the school founded in 1820 by missionaries, and of Cornell University's School of Hotel Administration, which had many graduates in positions of prominence in Hawaii's

When cane was king in Kaanapali, the original sugar train hauled recently cut cane to the mill in Lahaina, returning with molasses, which was shipped to California for processing. Today the train is a popular tourist attraction.

tourism industry. To be first in Hawaii's first planned destination resort would put a very large feather in his cap.

When plans for Kaanapali were announced, InterIsland was 85 years old, the modern descendant of an old steamship company with three hotels on the Big Island and Kauai.

Child negotiated a deal with Amfac to build a hotel on Black Rock, but his board of directors failed to support him, so the Sheraton went there instead. Another deal fell through a few years later for the site of what is now the Kaanapali Beach condominium.

Finally, in 1968, InterIsland marketed a new stock issue and with the money leased a third site from Amfac and entered into a joint venture development agreement with a big Mainland insurance company to build the first 250 rooms of the Maui Surf. Five years later, a second phase took the room count to 556.

By now, Amfac's resort was a great success. Hawaii achieved statehood in 1959, about the same time that groundbreaking began for the first Kaanapali hotel. As the number of Maui tourists increased, now there were hotels and condominiums to house them.

Lahaina was included in the master plan and improved. The cane-haul railway connection between Kaanapali and town was revived as a tourist attraction. The old Pioneer Inn was spruced up. A whaling ship was anchored at the dock and turned into a museum. Hundreds of new shops were opened for the tourist business and Lahaina was a boom town again.

By 1976, InterIsland was also a great success and again Dudley Child was encouraged to expand, planning to add a 200-room wing to his Maui hotel. It was not to happen. A combination of events and business reversals forced Child to liquidate. In 1985 the word went out: the Surf hotels were for sale.

Visitors to the Maui Surf Hotel had this open expanse of lawn to cross on their way to an empty beach. Today there are five swimming pools, two slides, several waterfalls, three restaurants and a small aviary of tropical birds.

Kaanapali Beach, 1987, with the Westin Maui under renovation in the center.

THE VISIONARY

Fantasy, Romance & Luxury

Hawaii was a new state when Christopher Bagwell Hemmeter stepped off the plane in 1960. He was from California, the son of an inventor. Like his father, he was a dreamer. Later, when some of his bigger dreams came true, the description would be upgraded to "visionary." He worked in Hawaii as a hotel management trainee during the summer of 1960, returning to permanently reside in the islands in 1962.

As a young man, Chris Hemmeter's dreams were mixed with ambition, and a desire to excel. At 10 years of age, he was earning as much as $400 a week selling Christmas cards door-to-door. In school, he was elected class president from the sixth grade through the twelfth and was student body president of his grammar school and high school. His athletic accomplishments were numerous, including letters in a variety of high school sports.

After earning a degree at Cornell University's School of Hotel Administration, Hemmeter took his dreams to Hawaii, which had been a state for just a year. It was, for the thousands who came flowing in, a golden land of opportunity—and for someone in that most idyllic of verbal contradictions, the "leisure industry," the sunniest new frontier.

After completing the Sheraton Hotel Corporation's two-year training program in six months, he became assistant manager of the Royal Hawaiian Hotel. When he resigned his position at the Royal Hawaiian 11 months later, he told his boss that he wanted to create his own hotel. The obvious response was, "Don't we all. But more importantly, how do you expect to accomplish this dream as a 24-year-old penniless lad?"

In 1964, with the help of his parents, Hemmeter borrowed $10,000 from the Bank of Hawaii to become a partner in a company established to develop restaurants in the Ilikai Hotel, then under construction. Two years later, he sold his interest in the business for a $14,000 profit and started another restaurant company, which he sold in 1968 for $1,500,000 in stock to a company which subsequently collapsed, rendering the stock worthless.

In the early 1970s, Hemmeter shifted his focus from restaurants to retail stores,

(Opposite page) A cluster of palms stands silent watch by a pool as still as night. The first lamps come on. The stars are on their way.

was what was called a "luxury visitor." An outside research firm hired by resort developers said it would be one out of four or five by 1990. These were people who were happy to pay more than double the statewide nightly room rate—a growing group of travelers who demanded much more than what Hemmeter disparagingly calls "a box and bed."

"We're creating monuments to mankind, to the joy of life, to the majesty of the senses. We want our visitors to hear the music, not just the lyrics. Our destination resorts are created to heighten one's fantasies, to bring back the romance of life. We attempt to restore the grandeur that King Louis XIV must have experienced at Versailles.

"We attempt to understand people's dreams and expectations and develop experiences that turn them on. We attempt to exceed those expectations. We want our architects to be psychologists who understand the dreams and motives of our guests and who can respond accordingly.

"Our design sessions revolve around discussion of dreams and fantasies of power and space, of romance and beauty, of plant life and animals, of art and culture, of quality and harmony and, oh by the way, of architecture!"

(Opposite page) Sitting at Cook's at the Beach, the visitor looks toward the pools nearby and sees a crane in the tropical growth. Is the crane real, or made of bronze?

Swans, the symbol of grace and elegance,
slide soundlessly across the pool at the Villas Restaurant.
They suddenly stop, and kiss.

The first seating at the Sound of the Falls Restaurant is about to begin. It is dusk, the twilight peace that follows the daily explosions of a Maui sunset.

An African Crown Crane sports a punk hairstyle beside a stately coco palm, seeming proud yet funny.

A pale, pink flamingo with an ebony beak adds to the sense of exotic romance.

Power and elegance march up these runway stairs
and past a Grecian colonnade,
disappearing into a golden tunnel of mystery.

In Northern China, near Mongolia, home of the Mongolian pony, this black marble horse was carved in the style of T'ang tomb figurines (618-906 A.D.). The large terracotta pot, originally used for carrying water in China, is now watered daily to keep the flowers bright.

Lacquered wood folding screens like this one were known in China as early as the 2nd Century B.C. As a piece of furniture, the screen provided privacy and offered protection from draft or the heat of a fire. As art, the possibilities were limitless.

This one has 12 panels and is in the style of the elaborate imperial palace screens. The classically garbed figures are shown on stylized clouds, reflecting some of the royal elegance of China in the 1600s and 1700s.

Ceramic Gods at Taoyuan Hsien

Yiu Ho-ki pulls an old book from a desk drawer in the employees' lounge on the second floor of the Twu Terng Ceramic Art Company factory in Taoyuan Hsien County, about 35 kilometers from Taipei.

Yiu is in his late 30s and is a recent arrival in Taiwan. Six months ago he lived in Hong Kong, where he studied—and worshipped—the ancient Chinese gods pictured in his book. He turns the pages respectfully, commenting in English on the artistic merits of the paintings and sculptures pictured. It is obvious that the book has been looked at frequently; the pages are cloth-like from use.

Yiu pulls a second book from the drawer. This one was written by his teacher, Cho Ming-lim; Cho's picture is opposite the title page. Yiu says proudly his teacher was born during the Ch'ing Dynasty, known for its superb ceramic craftsmanship. Yiu is proud of his artistic roots.

Yiu is one of 50 to 60 men and women who work in the firm's major plant, a three-level structure with concrete floors and a corrogated asbestos roof. The windows and doors are always open, making it bitterly damp and cold in winter, and damp and hot in summertime: never comfortable.

In China, ceramic vessels appeared as early as 5,000 B.C. Although many fine examples of ceramic ware have survived from these early times, most of what is seen today is from the Ming Dynasty (1368-1644), when so many blue-and-white porcelains were made, and from Yiu's revered Ch'ing Dynasty (1644-1911), when many other bright colors generally were added to the design.

The copies of ancient figures made by Yiu and his friends are sculpted from the same iron-free kaolinic clay used for centuries in China. Because the Republic of China (Taiwan) doesn't recognize the People's Republic of China, the kaoli is shipped in bags to Japan, and then is re-shipped to Taiwan, where it is mixed with water and then molded into giant vases and urns by hand.

Most of what is made here is far larger than what was made in the Ming and Ch'ing Dynasties. A couple of hundred years ago, a palace vase normally would be about 18 inches tall. For the Hemmeter hotels, the copies are nearly eight feet tall, on top of foot-high pedestals.

On each clay-colored level of the factory, artists carefully draw in pencil and then fill in and elaborate with paint the detailed figures of fish and dragons and dozens of other popular Chinese symbols, heroes and gods.

The larger pieces are fired in gas-heated kilns at 1,300 degrees Celsius (2,372 degrees Farenheit) for a period of three days. Smaller pieces are fired for 20 hours. The finished product is then inspected and packed in wooden crates for shipment by truck and sea.

The artists and artisans work steadily, quietly. The sounds are of a wheel turning as a scraper trims and smooths a giant fishbowl, and of the gas jets in the kiln (a modern dragon blowing his fiery breath).

There are simple kitchens, where fresh vegetables and tofu are cut and cooked in a steamy soup by some of the artists when it is time to eat. Shrines are nearby, with gifts of fruit and burning incense; the larger one pays homage to the traditional Chinese "triumvirate," the gods of Buddhism, Taoism and Confusianism, the smaller one to the red-faced god of war, Kuan-ti.

Thus, these men and women carve and mold and paint figures of their gods for export to the rest of the world, while in their place of work they worship them.

(Opposite page) Rows of vases made especially for the hotel stand waiting to be fired in a kiln in the countryside outside Taipei.

(Following pages) Yiu Ho-ki paints a mounted figure of the Chinese god of war, Kuan-ti, near Taipei.

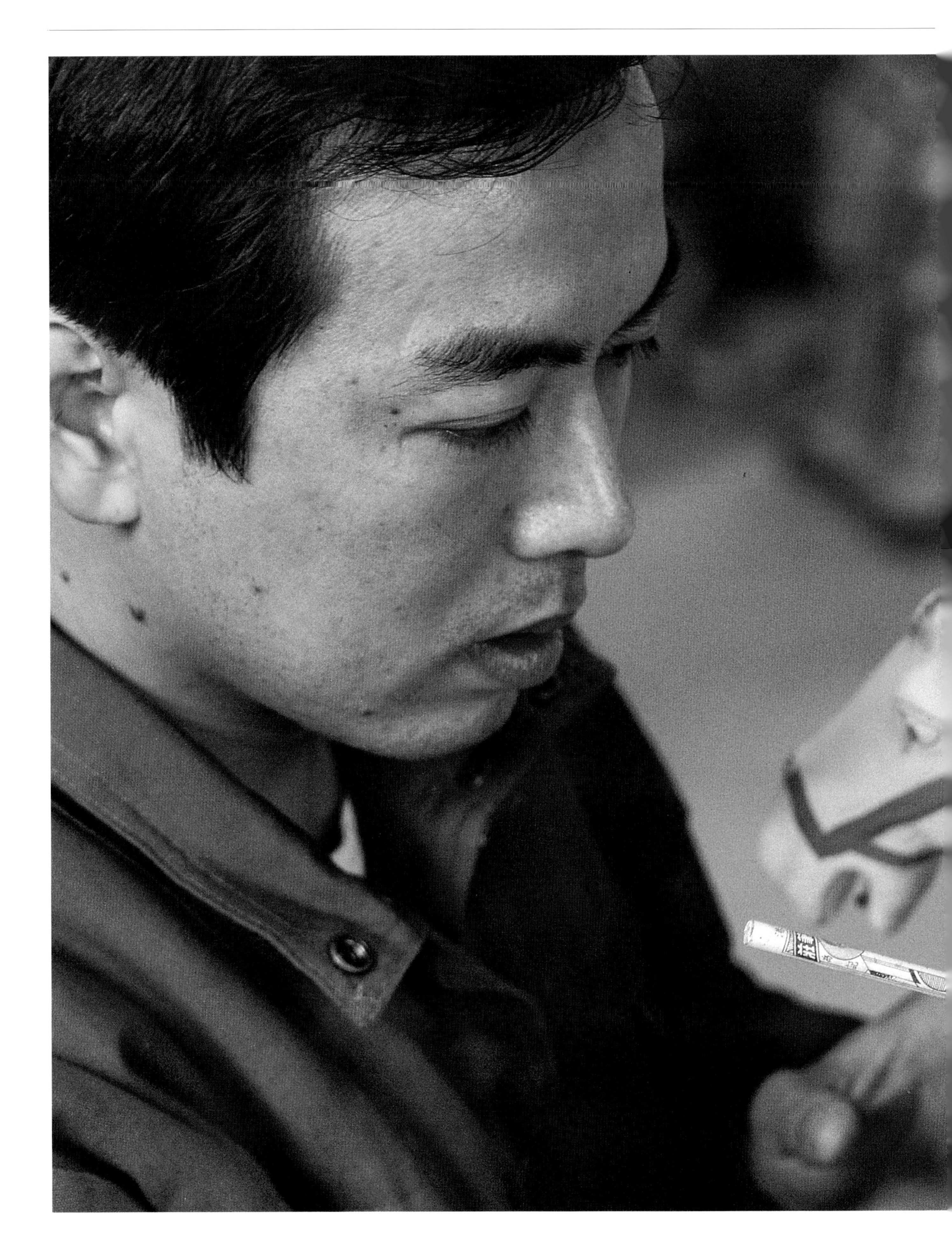

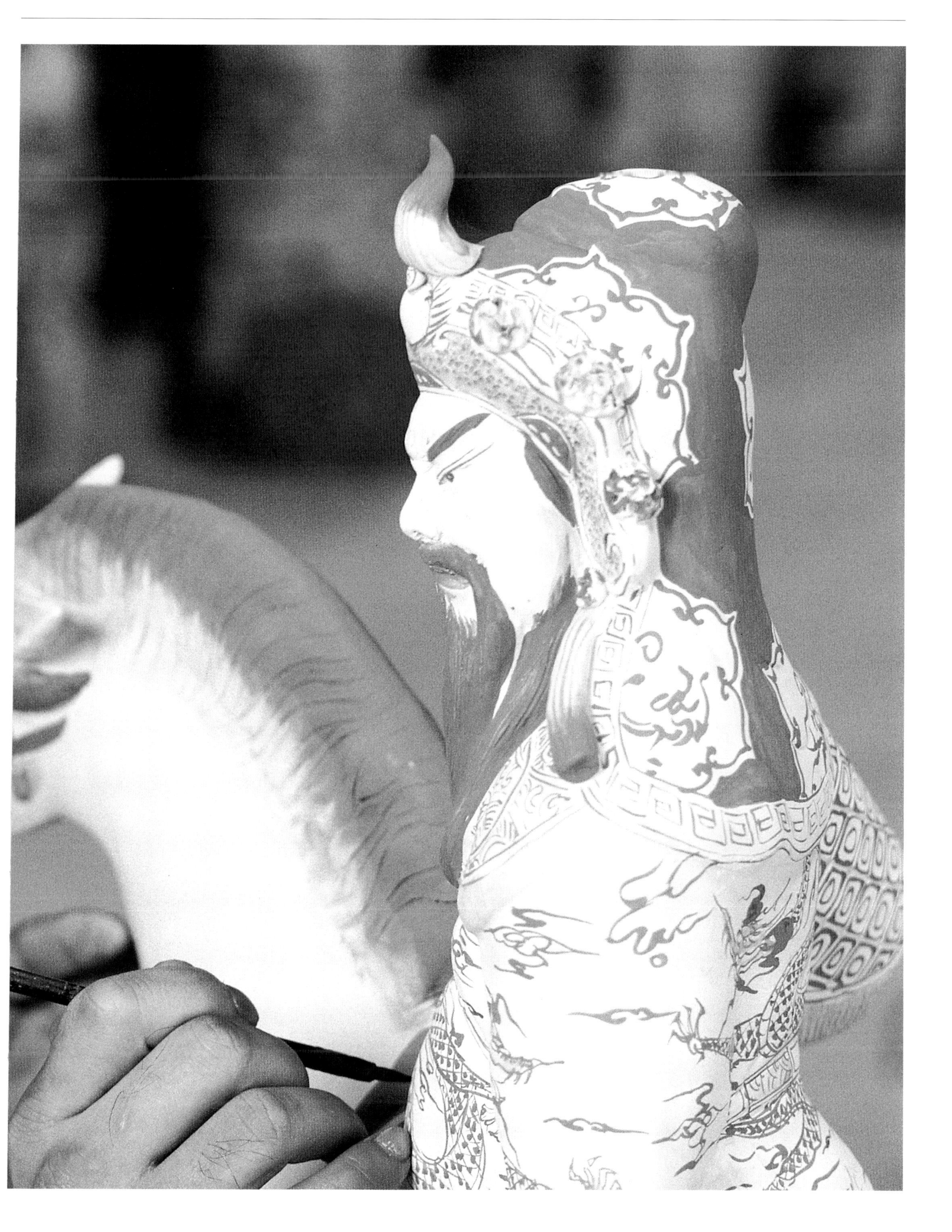

Oversized reproductions of 18-inch palace vases from the Ming and Ch'ing Dynasties of China are exhibited throughout the hotel.

(Opposite page) The blue and white ware, or imari, *are also produced in Japan, although all the ceramic art in the resort is from Taiwan or Hong Kong. The detail (opposite) shows a typical palace garden scene from the Ming Dynasty (1368-1644 A.D.). The more colorful vase (above) required additional overglazing with enamel which called for a second firing. The design reflects Buddha's love of flowers.*

(Following pages) This stylized guardian dog with cloven hooves, a protruding tongue, and a dragon's arrow-tipped tail, once stood in attendance outside of a temple in Thailand.

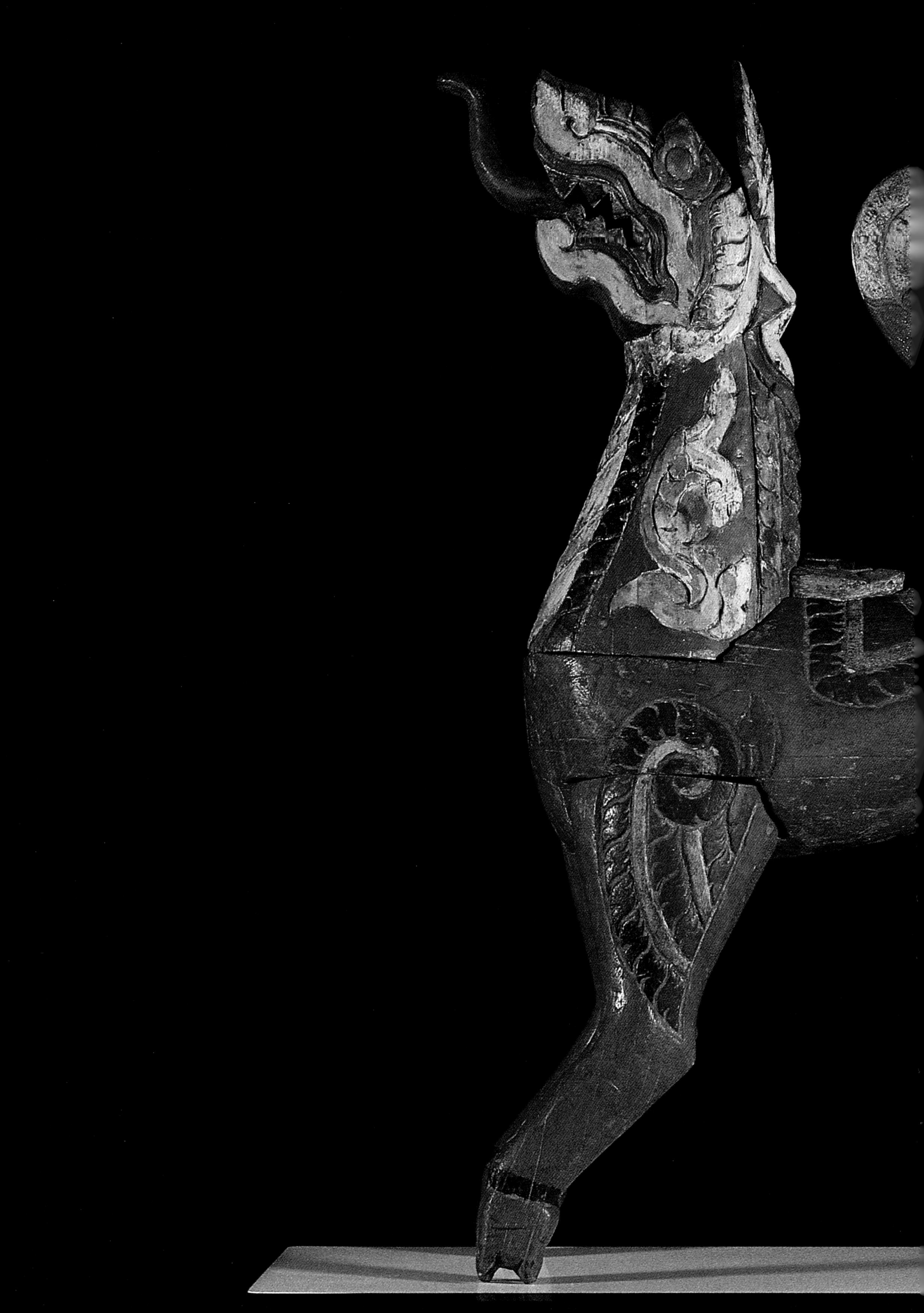

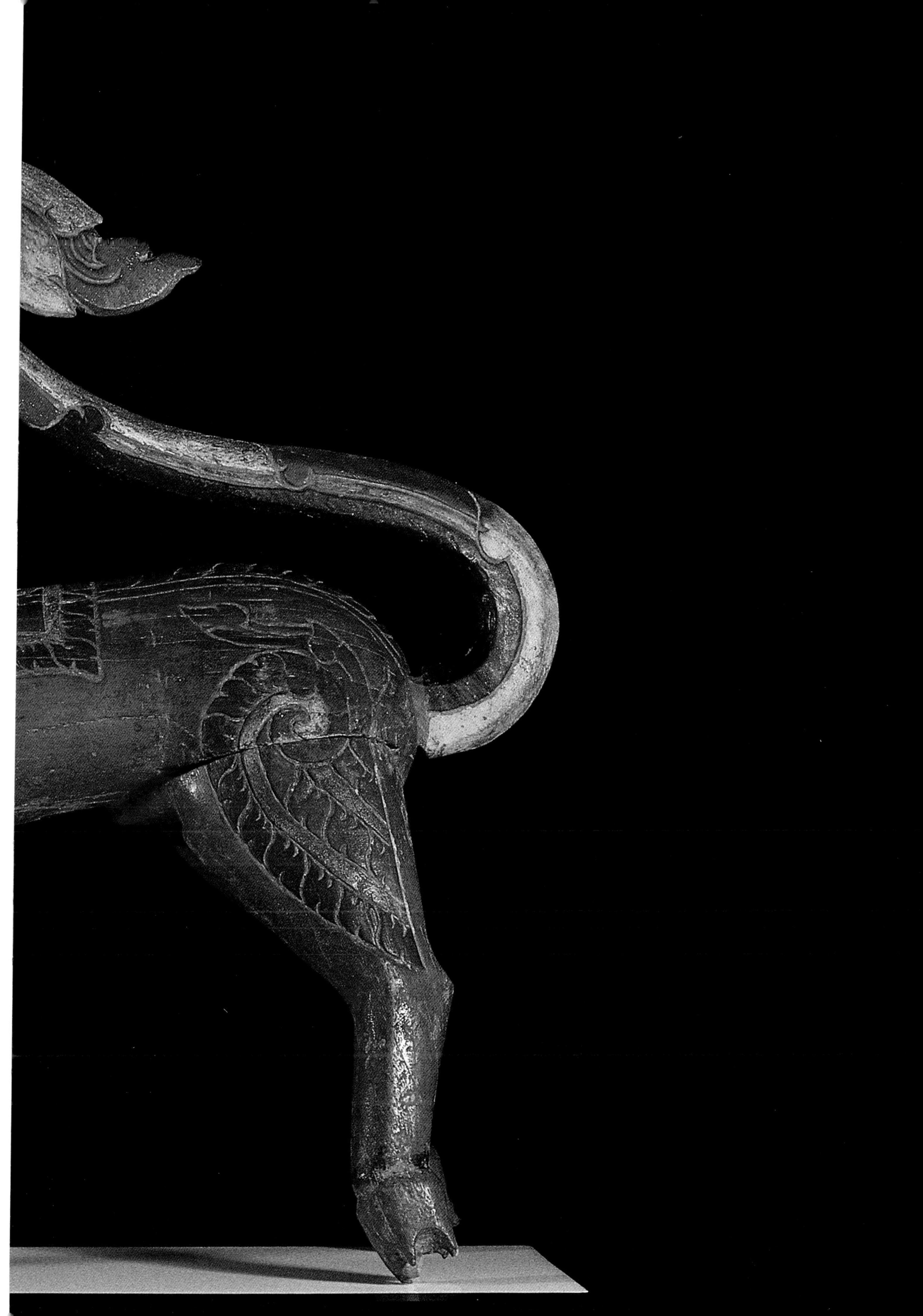

Two standing figures of bronze represent Vishnu, known as the "preserver," the second person in the Hindu trinity. (Brahma is the "creator," Siva the "destroyer.") The images, from Thailand, were cast in the style imported from India in the 8th and 9th Centuries.

(Opposite page) The elephant was sacred to Buddhists as a symbol of strength and wisdom, but also as one of the incarnations of Buddha himself. Buddha is also said to have accomplished the miraculous feat of throwing an elephant over a wall. The carved wood head in the colonnade area is from Thailand.

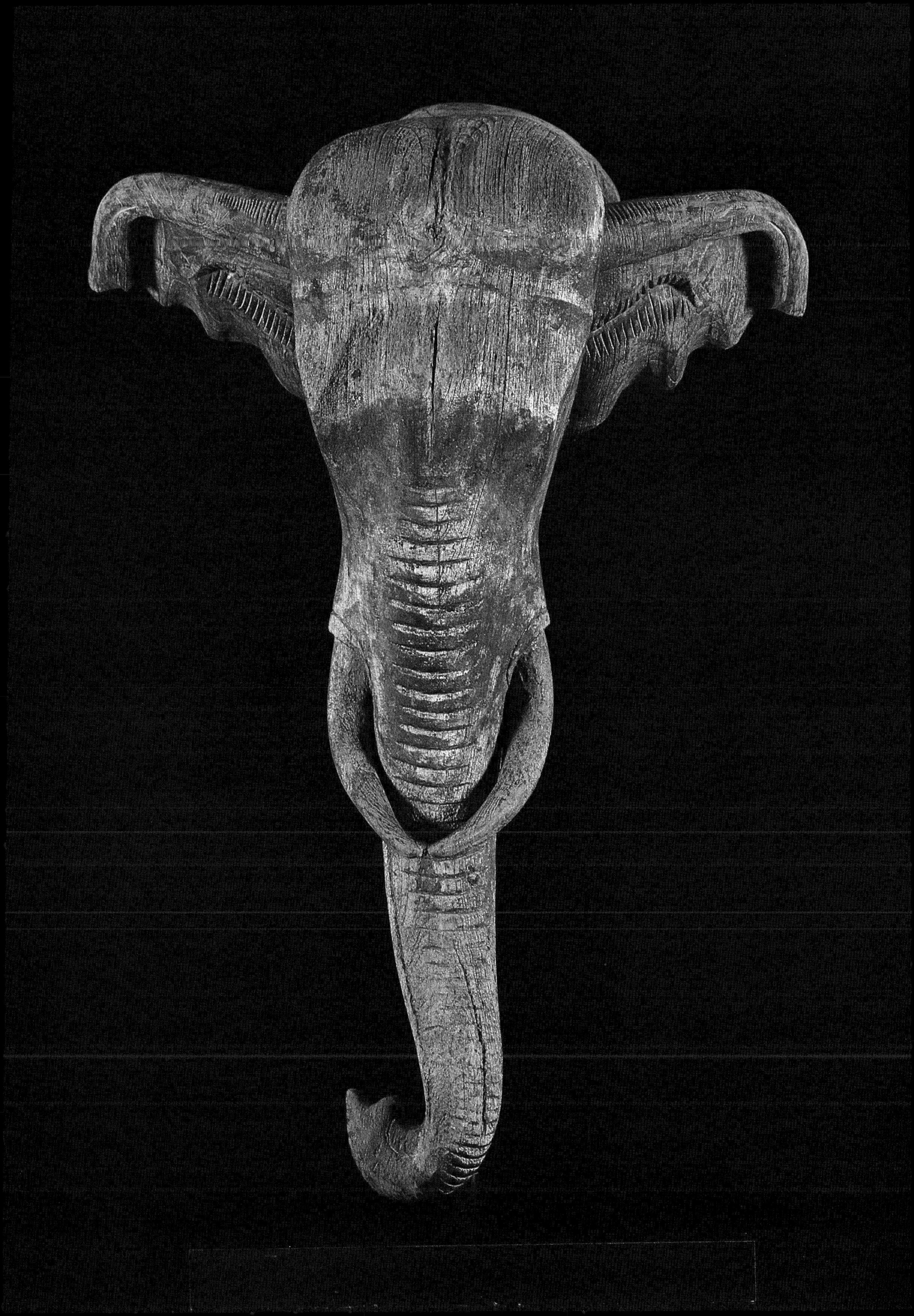

Thai mural paintings originally told stories about the previous lives of the Buddha, but now depict more commonplace scenes—such as this Bangkok river festival. The mural dates from the 19th Century.

Turning Motorcycles Into Art

In an open lot near the "factory's" main structure, the artists prepared to pour the molten bronze. It was dusk, getting dark. They lifted the heavy ladles and carefully filled the waiting molds, creating an extra-terrestrial glow in the fading Bangkok light.

The smell was pungent, like electrical wires sparking, mixed with the odor of melting wax. And the heat was blistering, causing the skin to bubble with protective sweat.

Bronze made of copper and tin is the oldest alloy known to man. People learned to make it about 4,000 B.C. The period in history between the Stone Age and the Iron Age is known as the Bronze Age because bronze was commonly used to cast containers such as cups, urns and vases. They also shaped bronze into battle axes, helmets, knives, shields and swords.

It is not cheap to make. Consequently, artisans in Thailand today are always looking for cost-saving shortcuts and imaginative sources. Cheaper lead is often added to the mix and at many workshops and factories, much of the metal is obtained by melting old motorcycle radiators.

Bronze is a favorite of sculptors because of its hardness and durability. Statues and bells made of bronze weather to a beautiful brown or develop a green patina (film) characteristic of copper. After such films form, bronze corrodes very slowly, so bronze articles frequently last hundreds of years.

Many such objects are exhibited in the Westin Maui. There are large, ornately decorated "rain drums" from Chiang Mai, so called because they are left in the garden to catch the thunder of the falling rain. There are European-styled statues baked to a golden brown. And there are greener bronze Buddha and guardian figures in the style found in Thailand's many temples.

All were made using the complex "lost-wax" process, which dates back to antiquity. (Much modern jewelery is also made this way.) First, the original figure is made, using any medium the artist chooses, then a "negative" mold is made from the figure, just as is done reproducing most sculptures.

At this stage, the process deviates, however. The inside of the mold is coated with a thin layer of wax, and the mold is filled with a mixture of plaster and sawdust. The whole thing is packed in clay and baked in high heat. This melts the wax, creating a space between the clay exterior and the plaster core.

This space is then filled with molten bronze and left to cool, after which the clay is carefully chipped away and the soft interior core is removed through a hole left in original mold. That hole is then patched and the finished piece is polished.

Thus has been created a thing of great beauty and strength—an object with thin skin which lends the extreme hardness of the metal a delicate sense of fragility.

(Opposite page) While exploring country roads in search of skilled artisans, the Hemmeters found a bronze factory where the molten metal is carefully poured into molds—creating an other-worldly glow.

(Following pages) A Thai artist pauses after creating a small Buddha figure, carved entirely from wax. A framed picture of his teacher is nearby, a constant reminder to strive for quality.

Across the river from Bangkok is the Wat Arun, or Temple of Dawn—the tallest in all of Thailand, its great, rounded chedi, *or spire, covered with pieces of porcelain contributed by Buddhist followers. Such temples are visited by the Hemmeters to see how the art was originally displayed.*

At the close of a long day collecting art, solitude comes with a traditional sunset visit to Wat Suan Doc in the northern city of Chaing Mai. The smaller chedi *contain ashes of the city's royal family and in the large central* chedi*, shown here, are no fewer than eight relics of the lord Buddha, or so the story goes.*

The artists are paid by how many pieces they produce and they share in their employer's profits, so the hours stretch into the night. Old paint buckets are used to hold the molds erect.

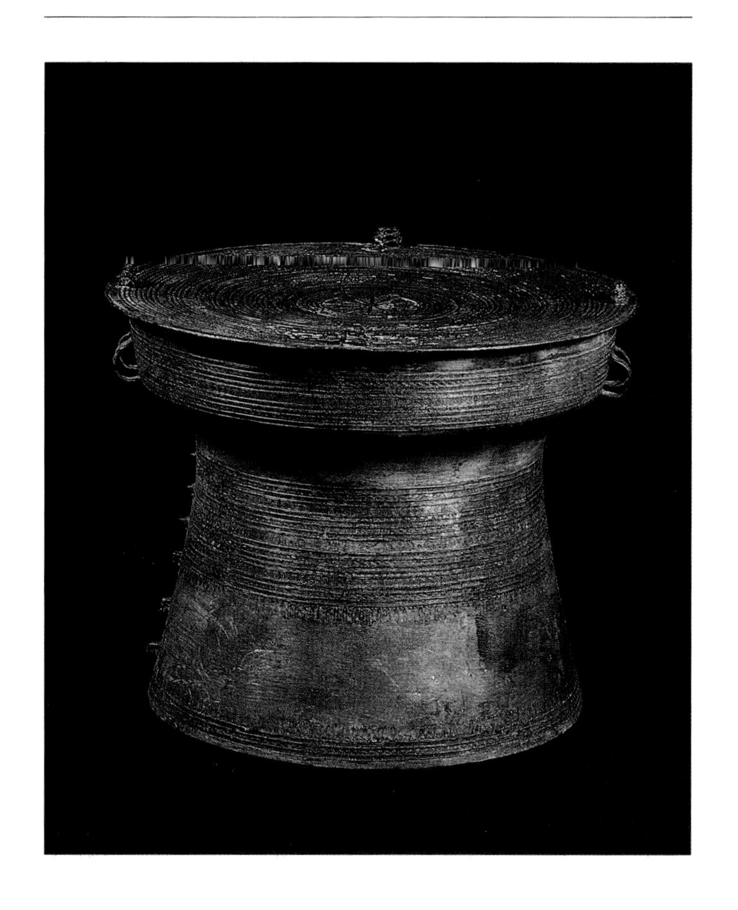

Large, ornately decorated "rain drums" from Thailand are so called because they are left in the garden to catch the patter and thunder of the falling rain. These thin-shelled creations, made in the ages-old "lost wax" method of bronze casting, are in use throughout the hotel as small tables.

(Opposite page) A detail from a carved wood temple shutter from Thailand shows a man against a lotus blossom motif. The full shutter reveals the figure standing on a dragon, holding a trident, the three-pronged spear that is one of China's classical symbols of power and authority.

Buddha's appearance and manner of adornment change from one country to the next. This bust (above), of carved and gilded wood, is from Thailand and it features a distinctive "flame-like" headdress.

(Opposite page) The fiercely scowling face, exaggerated musculature, and swirling ribbons of this guardian figure demonstrate a strength and ferocity that will defend the Buddha from evil demons. Although the figure was sculpted in northern China, it is modelled after a 30-foot figure which stands outside a temple in Japan.

The Chinese mix animal parts to blend the strengths of two or more animals into one. Lion-headed dragons like this one, carved from black marble, often are seen standing in pairs as guardian figures outside a temple or tomb.

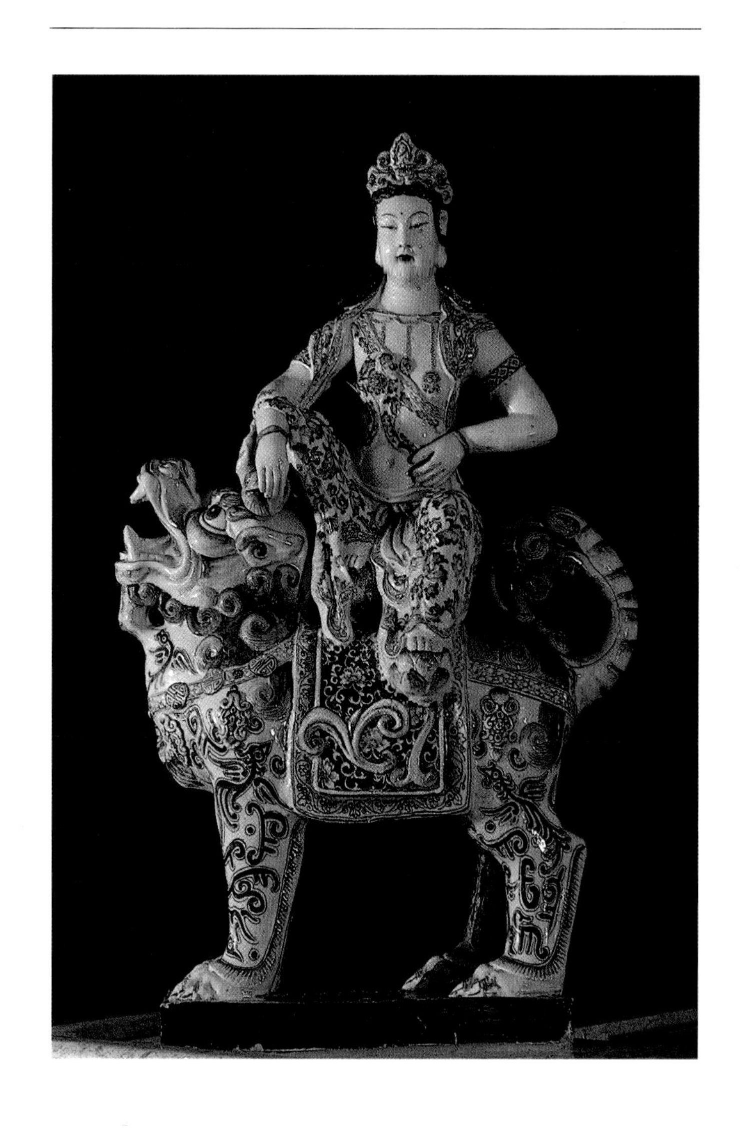

Emperors of the Ming Dynasty (1368-1644 A.D.) were known for their ostentatious tastes, building huge palaces and monuments and commissioning elaborate ceramic tributes to their gods like this one—a blue-and-white porcelain figure of Kuan Yin, seated astride a stylized guardian lion.

(Opposite page) Another Buddhist temple guardian, carved in China in black marble, depicts a lion's head atop a dragon's scaly neck.

(Following pages) The imperial power of the dragon is shown clearly in this elaborately carved lacquer table from Thailand. Throughout the East, the dragon is a popular symbol, representing the spirit of change, therefore of life itself.

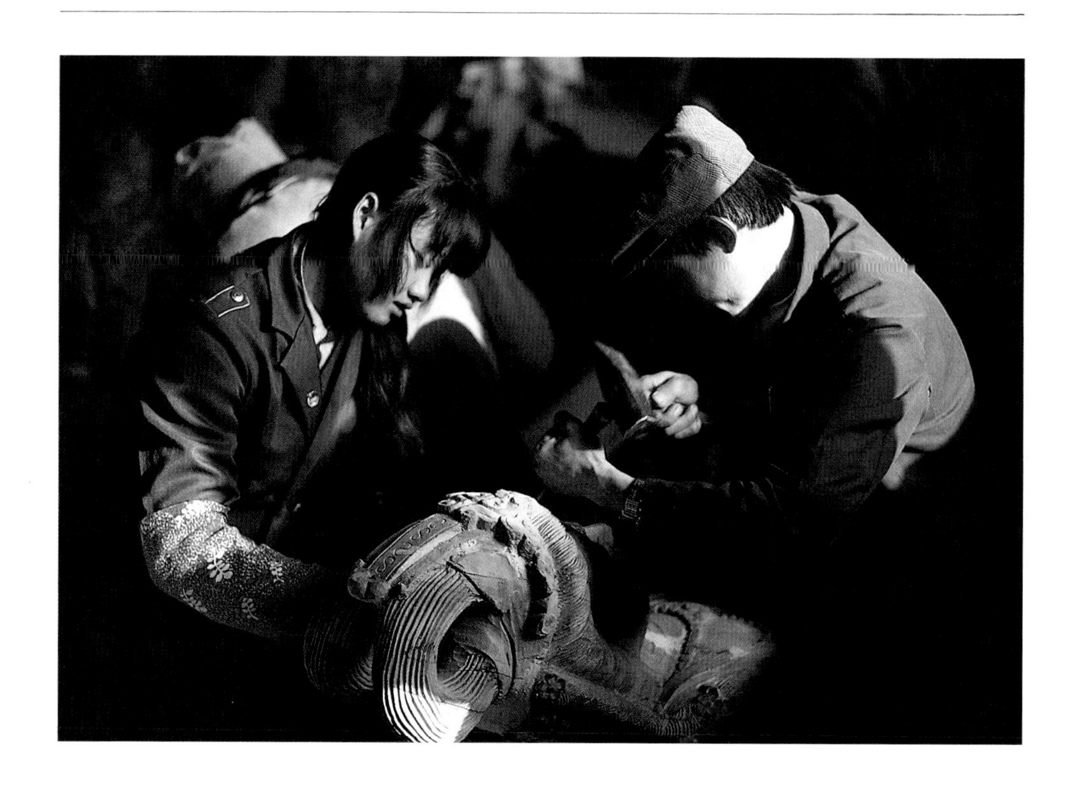

Families work together in the carving of China's treasured camphorwood. While the older workers wear the blue work clothes of the Communist revolution, the younger generation favors bright colors, not permitted in China until recently.

(Opposite page) A young man glues a block of wood to a figure's head, creating the raw material for a hat or elaborate hair style. Later, the figure will be polished and painted so that it looks as if it had been carved from a single piece of wood.

(Following pages) A donkey rests at the edge of the quarry, after handing a 1,000-pound block of bright white marble two long miles in a primitive two-wheeled cart to the "carving yard." Soon there will be another block of marble, then another, then another . . .

The Sensual Story of Kuan Yin

Kuan Yin is one of the most profound and revered figures in Buddhism, whose story is generally misunderstood.

Her origins in India are as a male figure called Avalokitisvara, born from a beam of light emanating from Buddha's eye. In India, as Buddhism was finding its early popularity, Avalokitisvara became known for his compassion.

Through many incarnations he lived, earning a place in nirvannah. Nonetheless, he turned away to return to the earth as a Bodhisattva to teach the Buddhist law—that there is a release from suffering—and the nature of that release.

The change in sexual identity and the name change to Kuan Yin occurred in China in the 7th Century. It also came about deliberately, when a priest translated the Indian name to mean "Hearer of the Sounds (of the cries of the world)." It was also said that, first in Tibet and then in China, a female deity of compassion was felt to be a necessity.

Whatever the reason, or cause, Avalokitisvara was now Kuan Yin, a male had become female, and the new, revitalized and redefined deity was at the center of a cult that included many non-Buddhists. Some even claimed she was a Taoist goddess.

Consequently, she was given great power and respect. She was compared, in later years, to the Virgin Mary. Young married couples prayed to her for children, pregnant women for sons, mothers for the health of those born.

Some say this identification with children coincided with the arrival in the Orient of the Portuguese, who brought Christian figures of the madonna and child. From this time forward, many figures of Kuan Yin included small children.

In China, her story sometimes is reduced to a simple folk tale, in which she defied her father's wish that she marry and was sent to a monastery where she was forced to cook and wash for 500 nuns. When her father heard that the birds and beasts did her chores for her, he burned the monastery and ordered her strangled.

There followed a period of time in the "world below." After that, came the Peace of Immortality and enthronement as Bodhisattva. Finally, when she heard of her father's terminal illness, curable only by a potion made from the eyes and hands of a living person, she plucked out one of her eyes and had her hands cut off. Her father was healed and thus became a Buddhist.

True believers are angered by such tales. Rightly, they cling to a more serious interpretation and point to the many symbols identified with the goddess. The lotus, known for its many seeds and consequent fruitfulness, frequently is included in the sculpture. So, too, the image of the pearl, which is regarded as the "concrete essence of the moon distilled through the secret workings of the Female Principle, Yin."

(Opposite page) Kuan Yin, the goddess of mercy, is shown with an elaborate hair style and a headband adorned with a lotus blossom. Yet, what shines through in this rose marble head from northern China is the character of the Sung Dynasty (960-1279 A.D.), when artists turned inward, becoming more contemplative, more spiritual.

The absolute purity of the goddess Kuan Yin is captured in white marble, in a poolside garden opposite Cook's at the Beach.

Large, elaborately carved mandalas like the one in the Sound of the Falls Lounge were commonly used as ceiling panels in Burmese temples—depicting the Buddhist "Wheel of Life (or Truth)." Just as a wheel crushes everything it passes over, the Buddha's teaching crushes all delusions and superstitions.

The resort grounds are painted in varied tones of tropical green, providing a soothing backdrop for bright flowers, such as this orchid, a member of the dendrobium *family.*

Throughout most of Asia, the fish is the symbol of wealth and abundance—a good thing, because these beautiful carp, or koi, today can cost as much as $50,000 apiece, depending on the color and size.

With Lanai in the distance, these hotel balconies, in precise alignment, stand ready to be filled with the gold of the setting sun.

Modern mariners are poised offshore, repeating a scene from ancient Hawaii, when canoes came into this beach. One fantasy ends. Another begins.

ACKNOWLEDGEMENTS

Robyn Buntin (Robyn Buntin of Honolulu) and Mary Snodgrass, for help in identifying and describing the Asian art.

Kepa Maly (Westin Kauai Resort) for providing so much information about the history and legend of old Hawaii.

W. Dudley Child, Jr. of InterIsland Resorts, for sharing memories and photographs.

Bernice Pauahi Bishop Museum, Lahaina Restoration Foundation, Hawaiian Mission Children's Society, Hawaii State Archives, Hawaii State Library, and Amfac, Inc., for assistance in historical research.

Kaanapali by Jodi Parry Belknap, © 1981 Amfac Property Corp. for information about early Kaanapali.

PHOTO CREDITS

Pages 35 & 36/37, Bernice Pauahi Bishop Museum; Pages 38, 41,42/43 & 44, Amfac/JMB Inc.; Page 40, Hawaii Mission Children's Society Library; Pages 46 & 47, Dudley Child; Pages 48/49, Media Systems, Inc.

Grand Resorts of the World logotype by Linda Fong.